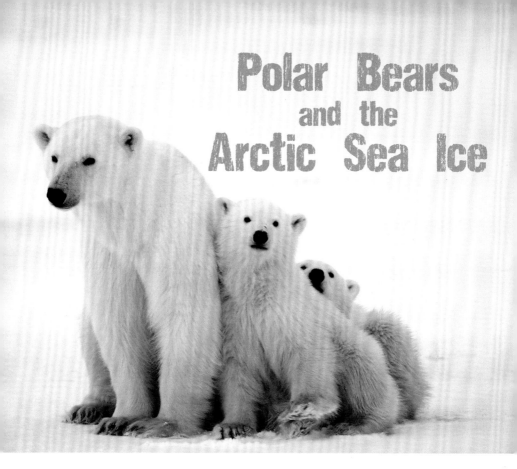

Polar Bears
and the
Arctic Sea Ice

Written by Max Greenslade

Flying Start
to Literacy®

Contents

Introduction

Arctic

Polar bears live in one of the coldest places on Earth. They live in the Arctic, which is the frozen northern part of the world.

Not many animals can survive in this harsh, frozen place, but polar bears can. They can find food and raise their young. The Arctic is their habitat.

Arctic fact

The Arctic includes the Arctic Ocean, which is surrounded by land.

In the past 100 years, the temperatures of the land and the sea on Earth have become warmer. These changes affect polar bears and threaten their habitat.

Arctic sea ice

The Arctic Ocean is the coldest ocean on Earth. It is so cold that part of the Arctic Ocean is covered in ice all year round. The ice is frozen sea water – it is sea ice.

Polar bears live on the sea ice close to the edge of the land. This is where they hunt for their food.

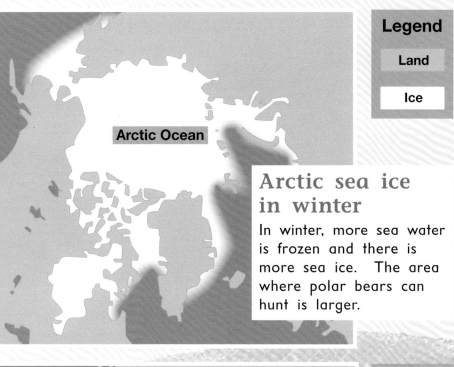

Arctic Ocean

Arctic sea ice in winter

In winter, more sea water is frozen and there is more sea ice. The area where polar bears can hunt is larger.

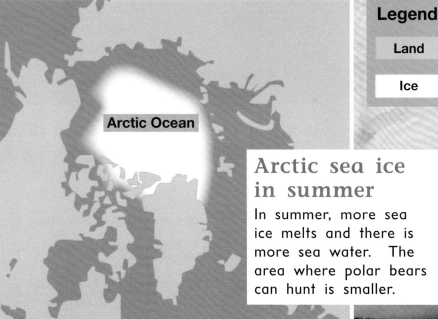

Arctic Ocean

Arctic sea ice in summer

In summer, more sea ice melts and there is more sea water. The area where polar bears can hunt is smaller.

Chapter 1

Living on the sea ice

Polar bears need to eat a lot of food to stay alive and to build up a thick layer of fat. This thick layer of fat keeps them warm.

Polar bears eat mainly seals. Seals have a thick layer of fat, which is called blubber. Blubber is high in fat. When a polar bear catches a seal, it mostly eats the blubber.

Hunting seals

Seals swim under the sea ice. Polar bears would need to swim for a long time under the sea ice to catch a seal. They cannot do this. Instead, polar bears hunt on top of the sea ice.

Polar bears travel long distances over the ice to hunt seals. They can smell seals under the ice. They find holes in the ice where the seals come up to breathe. They wait for the seals to come up for air, and then they catch them.

Arctic fact

Seals use their claws and teeth to make breathing holes in the ice. They dive through these holes and swim under the ice to feed. They use the holes to come up for air.

Winter food

In winter, the sea ice is very thick and covers most of the Arctic Ocean. It joins up to the edge of the land.

Polar bears travel over the sea ice to hunt seals all winter.

Arctic fact

Life in the Arctic is harsh. In winter, the temperature can drop to as low as -45 degrees Celsius, and it is dark all the time.

Summer food

In summer, polar bears live on the parts of the coast where the sea ice has not melted. If the sea ice melts and they get stranded on land, they cannot hunt seals.

On land, polar bears eat berries and bird eggs and hunt small animals. They have to compete with other animals for this food.

The food polar bears find on land does not give them the fat they need to stay warm.

Chapter 2

Raising a family

Female polar bears give birth to two or three cubs each year. They raise their young on the sea ice.

Digging a den

At the end of summer, the weather gets colder. Female polar bears dig a deep den in the snow. This is where they will give birth to their cubs.

Arctic fact

Polar bears, unlike other bear species, do not hibernate. Polar bear mothers are the only polar bears to spend the whole of winter in a den, where they look after their cubs.

Birth

Polar bear cubs are born in winter. They stay with their mother in the safety of their den all winter. They drink their mother's milk.

The mother polar bear does not eat all winter. She survives on her thick layer of fat.

Arctic fact

Polar bears can travel up to 30 kilometres a day to look for food.

Leaving the den

At the end of winter, mother polar bears and their cubs come out of their dens. The mother polar bears are very hungry because they have not eaten all winter.

The mother polar bears hunt seals on the sea ice straight away. They have to build up their body fat and they also have to teach their cubs how to hunt seals. They have to do this before the weather gets warm and the sea ice melts.

Chapter 3

A warmer Arctic

Today, there is less sea ice in the Arctic than ever before. This is because temperatures on Earth have become warmer and the sea ice is melting. Because they hunt on the sea ice, it is becoming harder for polar bears to find food and raise their young.

Longer summers

The sea ice that joins the land is melting earlier in summer. The sea water is freezing again later in winter. The polar bears have a longer time on land. They cannot reach the sea ice out at sea to hunt seals.

Also, less of the sea water is freezing again in winter. The area where polar bears can hunt in winter is getting smaller.

In summer, sea ice can break into large pieces of ice, which are called ice floes. Polar bears can swim between these floes. But when there is less sea ice, the ice floes are further apart. It is harder for polar bears to swim long distances and they can drown.

Hungry polar bears

When it is harder for polar bears to find food, they do not build up a thick layer of fat. If female polar bears cannot find food, they become too thin to have cubs.

When the sea ice melts earlier in summer, it is harder for mother polar bears and their cubs to hunt when they come out of their dens. The cubs will not grow as quickly. Cubs that are weak and small are less likely to survive.

Polar bears are in danger of becoming extinct.

Arctic fact

It is estimated
that there
are currently
20,000 to 25,000
polar bears.

Conclusion

Polar bears cannot live on land all year
round. They need the sea ice to survive
because this is where they find their food.

The food that the polar bears eat on land does not give them the fat that they need to stay warm and survive.

As the sea ice melts, the polar bears' Arctic habitat is changing. Polar bears might become extinct.

Glossary

blubber Some animals that live in the sea have a thick layer of fat to keep them warm. This layer of fat is called blubber.

compete Some animals have to be better than other animals to catch food to eat. They have to compete with other animals.

extinct When a group of animals dies out and no longer exists, it is extinct.

habitat The place where a group of animals lives and finds food is called a habitat.

ice floe A sheet of ice that floats on the sea is called an ice floe.

sea ice When the surface of the sea freezes, ice forms. This is sea ice.